A Thousand Paper Cranes

poems by

Megan Merchant

Finishing Line Press
Georgetown, Kentucky

A Thousand Paper Cranes

ACKNOWLEDGMENTS

I would like to extend gratitude to the editors and publications that first
published versions of these poems:

"A Thousand Cranes, A Wish", *Wild Horses*, 2016
"Consuming the Wick", *Crack the Spine*, Online. Summer 2015
"How to Fold an Origami Girl", *Wild Horses,* 2016
"Spitting Points", *One Sentence Poem*, December 30, 2015

Publisher: Leah Maines

Editor: Christen Kincaid

Cover Art: Joe Stepaniuk

Author Photo: Trisha Shaffer, Aris Affairs Photography

Cover Design: Elizabeth Maines McCleavy

Printed in the USA on acid-free paper.
Order online: www.finishinglinepress.com
also available on amazon.com

Author inquiries and mail orders:
Finishing Line Press
P. O. Box 1626
Georgetown, Kentucky 40324
U. S. A.

Table of Contents

Without a Knife

If two forks are resting
alongside a plate,
there will be a wedding.

If I leave my answer
nested in the rutted
veins of this paper,

there isn't another
who can read it
without undoing the
the lapsed wrinkles
and us knowing.

I offer this as a vow.

Please accept.

There is no way
to gape the heart
and keep salt
from thinning
onto the floor.

Any Given Day

To prepare the boat,

I pick a ring the swirling
color of ocean.

Hiking, a silver cross.

Church, blown glass and bruises.

There's only so much
I can prepare

without spoiling.

When he stands in the
doorframe,

I rouge.

A Thousand Cranes, A Wish

You are given a single piece of paper.

You cannot cut, or tab unwilling corners into place with glue.

You are told to make a wax moon, a perched swallow, a lamp.

You remember watching your mother rise from her bed, in an hour
that folded the light. The amber, rimpled sheets.

You remember that shadows are seamless.
You cannot be haunted by fragments.

You want the center to announce itself. To yaw the way
still water undresses for a body. To ruffle outward. To filigree.

You remember how she slept, the thinnest sheet resting over her face.

A crocus.

The slender silk of spring, damp-tapered leaves and scrub.

Love Note

Scabbed seam
where you carelessly
folded my legs
underneath
so I'd crumple
into your pocket.

Morning Sleeve

Tell me again
the morning light
is an orchid
in the crosshairs of a falcon
and surging stream.

Tell me
that my weather-blissed
skin is a juniper
moon—
pale, cooled,
brushed with talcum.

Teach me
how to pull
the soul from
its sleeve
by beading a hymn
of birdsong,

knotting tall grass
around its pulse,

and how the new-hatched
rattled-breath
hasn't learned restraint,

is curled on a warming rock
sleeping,

is a prayer of caution.

A Single Glass of Wine

A quaver rest
behind my tongue
where you draped
your words
damply
over mine.

Stay.

And I crouched
into *yes.*

How to Fold an Origami Girl

Glue the hair on her popsicle stick neck.
Trim any wisps from straying.

Rub dark cherry juice on her mouth and cheeks,
blush underneath her floral skirt.

Give her words that ripen, forget to explain
how heat will bruise and wilt—

the grip of a man's hand, the pressure of his ribs
over hers. Let spoiling be a surprise.

Cut sleeves that look like pie-sliced wings from behind—
awkward angles, too wide for a doorframe.

Tuck them precisely under her edges.
Shave her hips, but make her visible enough

to navigate crowds, slackened enough to warrant
attention. Shade her eyes dinner-table-polite,

grey-blot a shadow so she has an anthem. Tear a corner,
make her damaged enough to be an incandescent attraction,

a fat-lettered sign with flickering bulbs. Take away her vowels
so she has to find her strength in consonants stable enough

to crux a wing, then add a dimmer switch, so she blends, is not
the brightest hue in the room.

Once she is erected and primed, she can chose her use—
a vase for the ocean, or a cup for salt.

Splitting Points

The lightest rain
in heat
is sweat,

glistens
and wrinkles
the paper-brick house
we kept dark
so as not
to singe
the joints.

Before the After of You

How to fold and unfold,
to leave
a crease—

Braille instructions
passed from tongue to tongue.

How I like the splaying lotus
best,

red, below the sympathy
of muted stars.

Kusudama

They are everywhere—
the girls you've known,
soft Washi paper
petals sewn together
by their sharpest points
to make a curious,
glowing ball.

You hang them
in our hallway
and my countdown
begins,

every time
you pass
through the door
until the day
I blur
and you see fit
to string me up
alongside.

To be invisible is to be seamless.

I could turn a key,
slip a lock,
slide into your furrowed bed—

satin sex-sheets spritzed
with body spray like a coat
of armor,

      and you would
never know.

Not in a creepy,
stalker way.

In a growing   invisible
kind of way.

I could sprawl out a billboard
of sex-pot legs,
         arch into a bridge
of breasts and sculpted hedge

and you'd start thinking about
therapy,

the gluey gunk on the
floor of our minivan,

what's for dinner.

I forgot to bless

the last time
someone looked at me

as something to pry open,
kneel before and hum.

Way Station

We are monarchs and the girl
        in the middle has milkweed hair.

Her hands are sober— wisdom mudras
        perching on the thin wire of time.

She hums. My legs are a skyline of tin roofs,
        mouth of cardboard houses sagging in the rain.

When the earthquake comes, there will be rubble,
        piles of metal chairs, split, untucked seeds

and the pinstripe moon will drip tar,
        pinking scars onto our skin—

proof that we are not strung paper,
        but feathered stones, wings bunched in sediment.

Rain Doll

Little pale, bald ghosts
strung
in the window.

You have it all wrong—
they are not warding
off drab weather,

theirs is an invitation
for brightness.

You ache
before the dampness
even sinks
between the split
wood slats,
you creak.

Pacing the hall
to keep me from sleeping,
to slay me
for not stopping
at *enough*.

Things I want to tell you, still.

My heart is wrapped in wet muslin.

I slipped floats of thistledown
into a mason jar with a white tea light,
called it a *thrum*, a *lisp*, a *benediction*.

Some nights the cicadas rub
the quick-way you said my name.

The spoons clatter, then repose.

If I hold my head under water past the struggle,
my body starts to believe it too doesn't need air,
that it could visit and make friends with roots
that have vined your bones,

watch the spectacular show, the galaxy of cells
bursting and maggots, like little balloons of happy,
getting fat on your skin and hair.

I miss the way sadness used to be fragile,
how it would float and skim.

Grief sunk the smell of parceled sod into my sheets,
iron under my tongue.

Blue-black fingers lace my sleep in patterns,
fly-wings lash the air and I think you sent them, maybe.
When I wake, they are never there.

The morning glare over your coffee cup
is the lisp in the light.

I paginate leaves along the path to your grave,
so the wind knows where to pause and how to
pay its respects.

Consuming the Wick

A monarch floats
by the open door,
flimsy as memory.

I swear, as a girl,
there were hundreds
of summery stick-wings
like walking plows
turning the air
in our backyard,

and when they scattered,
the edges of sky torched
and frayed.

To nearly touch

the dent
his head
makes
on the pillow
that smells
like tangerine
and fur,

is to blur
the soft
edges
between
familiar
and worn.

Humming Bee

The close taste
that unwinds on
your lips
before swallowing.

Trying to hide
the stung panic
once its gone.

Megan Merchant is a Prescott resident and holds a Master of Fine Arts degree from UNLV. She is a multi-year Pushcart Prize nominee, and her poem, "Filling Station God" won the Las Vegas Poets Prize, judged by Tony Hoagland. Her second full-length collection,"The Dark's Humming" was the winner of the 2015 Lyrebird Prize (Glass Lyre Press, 2017).

She is also the author of four chapbooks: *Translucent, sealed.* (Dancing Girl Press, 2015), *In the Rooms of a Tiny House* (ELJ Publications, October 2016), *Unspeakable Light* (Throwback Books, August 2016), and *A Thousand Paper Cranes* (Finishing Line Press). *Gravel Ghosts* is her debut full-length poetry collection through Glass Lyre Press.

She also has a children's book forthcoming through Philomel Books.

You can find her work at meganmerchant.wix.com/poet.

www.ingramcontent.com/pod-product-compliance
Lightning Source LLC
LaVergne TN
LVHW021129080426
835510LV00021B/3367